BIG BEASTS
Gorilla

**Stephanie
Turnbull**

Published by Smart Apple Media
P.O. Box 1329
Mankato, MN 56002

Printed in the United States of America,
at Corporate Graphics in North Mankato, Minnesota.

Designed by Hel James
Edited by Mary-Jane Wilkins

Library of Congress Cataloging-in-Publication Data

Turnbull, Stephanie.
   Gorilla / Steph Turnbull.
      p. cm. -- (Big beasts)
   Includes index.
   Summary: "An introduction on gorillas, the big beasts in Africa.
Describes how gorillas move, find food, communicate, and care
for their young"--Provided by publisher.
   ISBN 978-1-59920-835-0 (hardcover : library bound)
   1. Gorilla--Juvenile literature. I. Title.
   QL737.P96T865 2013
   599.884--dc23

                     2012004114

Photo acknowledgements
l = left, r = right; t = top, b = bottom, c = center
page 1 Eric Isselée/Shutterstock; 3 emin kuliyev/Shutterstock.com;
4 Jacek Jasinski/Shutterstock; 5 iStockphoto/Thinkstock;
6 iStockphoto/Thinkstock; 7 Bruce Davidson/Nature Picture
Library; 8 iPics/Shutterstock; 9 Hemera/Thinkstock; 10 Sam
DCruz/Shutterstock; 11 FAUP/Shutterstock; 12 Stockbyte/
Thinkstock; 13 emin kuliyev/Shutterstock; 14 Anup Shah/
Thinkstock; 15 iStockphoto/Thinkstock; 16 emin kuliyev/
Shutterstock; 17, 18, 19, 20b Eric Gevaert/Shutterstock,
20t iStockphoto/Thinkstock; 21 Eric Baccega/Nature Picture
Library; 22t Eric Isselée/Shutterstock, b Nattika/Shutterstock;
23t oorka/Shutterstock, b NMorozova/Shutterstock
Cover Eric Isselée/Shutterstock

DAD0503a
112012
9 8 7 6 5 4 3 2

Contents

Gentle Giants 4

Gorilla Homes 6

Follow the Leader 8

Finding Food 10

Yawn! 12

Watch Out! 14

Gorilla Babies 16

Growing Up 18

Gorilla Talk 20

BIG Facts 22

Useful Words 23

Index 24

Gorillas are
massive!

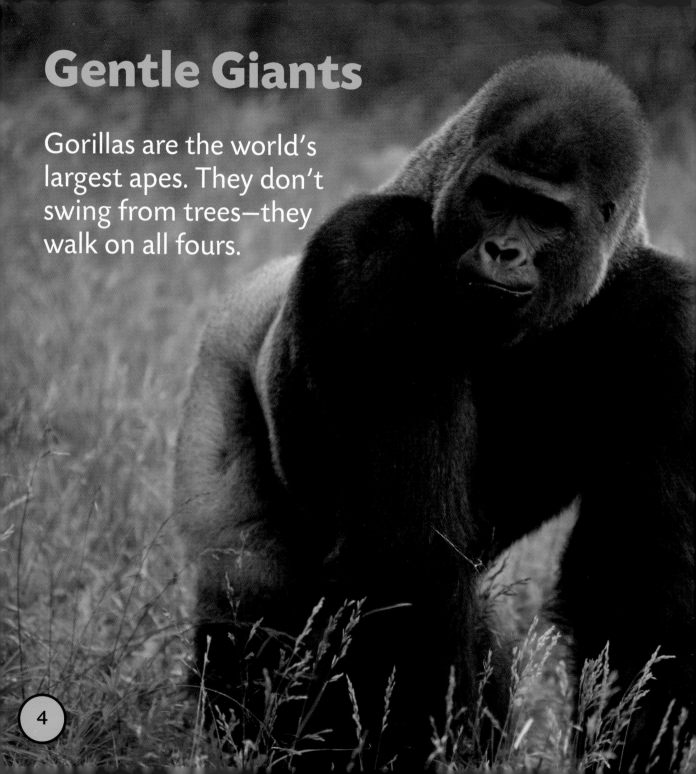

Gentle Giants

Gorillas are the world's largest apes. They don't swing from trees—they walk on all fours.

4

Gorillas may
look fierce, but
they are really
very peaceful,
shy animals.

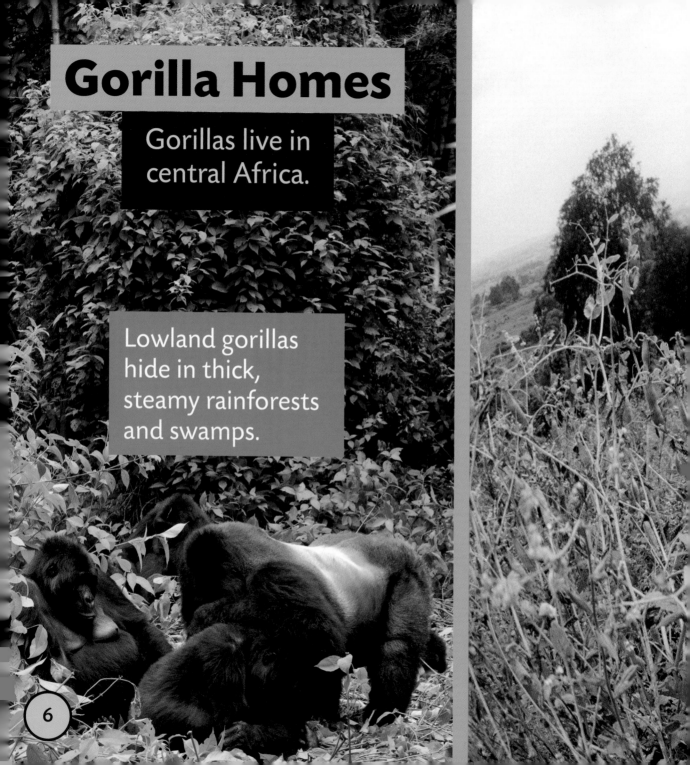

Gorilla Homes

Gorillas live in central Africa.

Lowland gorillas hide in thick, steamy rainforests and swamps.

Mountain gorillas roam in high, misty mountains. Extra-thick hair keeps them warm.

7

Follow the Leader

Gorillas live in groups called troops.

Each troop has mothers, babies, young gorillas, and one huge male. He is called a silverback because of his silvery hair.

The silverback is the big boss. He leads the group.

9

Finding Food

Gorilla troops spend the day looking for tasty plants to eat.

They munch leaves and grind up tough stalks with their big, strong teeth.

Sometimes gorillas eat fruit or ants.

Yawn!

When gorillas aren't eating, they like to lie back and relax.

At night, they build nests in trees, using branches and leaves.

Babies snuggle up with their mom.

The heaviest gorillas stay on the ground.

Watch Out!

Sometimes leopards or other silverbacks
try to attack a gorilla troop.

This makes the silverback angry!

To scare enemies away, he stands tall and **THUMPS** his chest. He rips up plants, hoots, and slaps the ground.

15

Gorilla Babies

Female gorillas have one baby every few years.

Newborn babies are tiny and weak. They drink their mother's milk and stay close to her.

Soon they are able to ride on their mother's back.

Growing Up

Gorilla babies start to explore on their own. They love to run, tumble, and play with other babies.

When males are about 11, their hair begins to turn silvery. Soon they will leave the troop.

Gorilla Talk

Gorillas are smart animals that like to talk to each other.

GRUFF... GRUFF

Deep, rumbling burps mean, "I'm happy!"

Grunts and barks mean, "Where are you?" or, "Come here!"

Buuuuuuuuurp

Screams and roars mean, "Watch out— danger!"

RAAARR!

BIG Facts

Big gorillas can hold out their arms wider than you and a friend laid end to end.

Every day, gorillas eat food that weighs as much as 120 potatoes.

Silverbacks are about ten times stronger than an adult human.

Gorillas can be as heavy as a big piano.

Useful Words

ape
A large, tail-less animal, such as a gorilla, chimpanzee, gibbon, or orangutan.

silverback
A fully-grown male gorilla.

troop
A family group of gorillas. There are often about ten gorillas in a troop.

Index

babies 9, 13, 16, 17, 18, 19

food 10, 11, 22

hair 7, 9, 19
homes 6, 7

nests 13

silverbacks 9, 14, 15, 22
size 3, 4, 9, 22

talking 20, 21
teeth 10
troops 8, 9, 10, 14, 19

Web Link
Go to this website for mountain gorilla facts, photos and a video: http://kids.nationalgeographic.com/kids/animals/creaturefeature/mountain-gorilla